Contents

INTRODUCTION

TV's can come in all shapes colours and sizes but they all do the same thing - provide us with entertainment.

For those of us who grew up with no TV's, the world of technology can be frightening.

You can fix the TV yourself, you have just not been taught!

This guide is here to show you that using your TV and fixing the issues yourself do not need to be scary and once you learn the basic in's and out's you will be feeling much more confident in your abilities.

REMEMBER: You cannot break the TV by pressing the wrong button. Anything that goes wrong, you can easily fix by knowing what buttons to press.

You are not alone in your TV struggles, many people do not know how to fix issues as they have never been taught. I hope this book becomes a friend to you in fixing your TV issues and has you feeling like a superhero!

Chapter 1: Using the Remote

Your TV remote might look different from someone else's, but don't worry. All remotes work in similar ways and have the same basic functions. Let's start by understanding the most important buttons and how to use them.

Getting to Know Your Remote

TV remotes come in all shapes and sizes. Some have lots of buttons, while others are simpler.

Even though they may look different, all remotes do the same things: turn the TV on and off, change the volume, switch channels, and navigate menus.

The colour's and shapes of the buttons on your TV remote do not matter and it may be different from ones you have seen before.

When using the remote, focus on what the writing or icon on the button says. If you take time to read and look at what is on your remote, you will become more familiar!

To Begin with we are going to focus on the main buttons:

- POWER ON / OFF
- VOLUME
- CHANGE CHANNELS
- MUTE
- Menu

Here are the buttons you will use most often:

Power Button: This turns your TV on and off. It is usually at the top of the remote and marked with a small circle and a line like this:

Volume Buttons: These make the sound louder or quieter. Look for "+" to turn the volume up and "-" to turn it down.

Channel Buttons: These let you move up and down through the channels. They are often marked with "CH +" and "CH -."

Mute Button: This turns the sound off completely. It usually looks like a speaker with a line or cross through it.

Menu Button: This opens a list of options on your TV screen, like picture settings or input sources. It might say "Menu" or have three horizontal lines.

4

Using the Buttons

Turning the TV On and Off

1. Point the remote at the TV.
2. Press the Power Button once to turn the TV on.
3. Press it again to turn the TV off. It's that simple!

Adjusting the Volume

1. Press the Volume + button to make the sound louder.
2. Press the Volume - button to make it quieter.
3. If you don't want any sound, press the Mute Button. To turn it back on, press the mute button again.
4. Press it again to bring the sound back.

Changing Channels

Use the CH + button to move to the next channel.

Use the CH - button to go back to the previous channel.

What If Your Remote Has Extra Buttons?

Don't worry if your remote has buttons you don't understand. You don't need to use all of them right away.

Focus on the basics: Power, Volume, and Channels. Once you feel more comfortable, you can learn about the other buttons.

Troubleshooting Your Remote:
Sometimes the remote might not work. Here's what you can try:

Check the Batteries:
If the remote isn't working, the batteries might need to be replaced. Look for a small cover on the back of the remote, slide it open, and change the batteries.

Point It at the TV:
Make sure there's nothing blocking the signal between the remote and the TV.

Press Buttons Gently:
Sometimes pressing too hard can damage the buttons. A light press is enough.

Practice Makes Perfect

Take some time to practice with your remote.

Turn the TV on and off, adjust the volume, and switch channels.
The more you use it, the easier it will feel.
Remember, it's okay to make mistakes. You can always try again!

Chapter 2: What Are All the Things That Plug Into My TV?

When you look at the back of your TV, you might see lots of holes and plugs. It can seem confusing, but it's actually quite simple once you know what each one is for. Let's break it down step by step.

The Common Types of Plugs

Power Cord:

This is the most important plug. It's where your TV gets its electricity.

The power cord goes into the wall outlet and normally plugs in at the back of your tv.

It will be a thick cable that has an end that will go into your wall plug socket.

HDMI Ports:

These are small, flat slots usually labelled "HDMI."

They are used to connect devices like streaming boxes (e.g., Virgin Media, SKY, any tv box or Fire Stick), DVD players, or game consoles.

Plugging it in connects the gadget by sending the signal to the TV.

If you're plugging in something and it doesn't fit, check if it's an HDMI cable—it only fits one way.

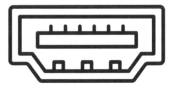

The slot to plug in looks like this.

The shape at the end of the wire will fit in to the above.

USB Ports:

These look like the ports on a computer for plugging in flash drives or charging cables.

Sometimes, they're used for devices like a streaming stick or for viewing photos and videos from a USB drive.

This is the least used connection on a TV.

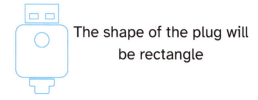

The shape of the plug will be rectangle

Cable or Antenna Port:

This is a round hole where you can plug in a cable or antenna.
It's used if you watch regular TV channels through an antenna or cable service.

Audio Ports:

These are small round holes.

They're used for speakers, headphones, or soundbars to improve your TV's sound.

What Do These Devices Do?

Here are some common devices you might plug into your TV:

TV Boxes, Streaming Boxes or Sticks: These let you watch Netflix, YouTube, or other apps.

DVD/Blu-ray Players: For watching movies on discs.

Game Consoles: Like PlayStation or Xbox for playing video games.

Soundbars: To make the sound louder and clearer.

Antennas: For watching free over-the-air channels like local news.

Don't Worry About Making Mistakes

It's okay to feel unsure at first. Most devices and cables only fit in one spot, so it's hard to plug them in wrong. If something doesn't work, you can always unplug it and try again, it will not break anything.

In the next chapter, we'll learn how to find the right channel or input for whatever device you've plugged in. You're doing great so far—keep going!

Chapter 3: Finding a Channel

Now that you know how to use your remote and what might be plugged into your TV, let's learn how to find a channel to watch. Don't worry—this is easier than it might seem!

THIS IS FOR USING REGULAR FREE CHANNELS - If you are using a TV box (Sky, Virgin Media, Something that has more channels than free to air channels, turn to next page.

Using the Channel Buttons
Most remotes have buttons that say CH+ (Channel Up) and CH- (Channel Down).
Press CH+ to move to the next channel.
Press CH- to go back to the previous channel.
Keep pressing until you find something you want to watch.

Entering a Channel Number
If you know the channel number, you can type it directly using the number buttons on your remote.
For example, press 2 and then Enter (or OK) to go to Channel 2.

Using the TV Guide
Some TVs and remotes have a Guide button.
 This shows a list of all available channels and what's playing.
1. Look for a button that says Guide or Menu. If you press the wrong button press it again to return to normal.
2. Use the arrow buttons to scroll through the list.

Highlight a channel or show and press OK or Enter to select it.

Switching Between Regular TV and Plugged-In Devices

If you have a streaming box (TV box), DVD player, or other device plugged in, you need to switch to the correct Input or Source to use it. Do this by using the TV remote that controls the TV, not the box you are trying to connect.

Look for a button on your remote that says Input, Source, or AV. It will look like the button below:

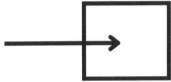

Press it, and a list of options will appear on the screen.
Use the arrow buttons to highlight the right option (like HDMI 1, HDMI 2, or TV) and press OK.

If you're not sure which input to choose, try each one until you see what you want on the screen.

What If Nothing Happens?
Make sure the device is turned on (like your streaming box or DVD player).

Double-check the cables to ensure they're plugged in securely.

Chapter 4: Using a Plug-In TV Box

If you've plugged in a TV box like a Roku, Amazon Fire Stick, Apple TV, or another streaming device, this chapter will help you use it with ease.

These devices let you watch more TV channels or access streaming apps like Netflix, YouTube, or Disney+ and give you access to many more shows and movies.

Setting Up the TV Box
1. Plug It In:
 Connect the device to an HDMI port on your TV.

Plug the device's power cable into a wall outlet.

2. Switch to the Right Input:

Press the Input or Source button on your TV remote (the remote that controls the TV, not boxes or sticks connected.)

Select the HDMI port where your box is plugged in (e.g., HDMI 1 or HDMI 2).

Once set-up Follow On-Screen Instructions:

When the box is connected, you'll see setup instructions on the screen.

Move the screen by pressing the arrow buttons (up, down, left or right)

You cannot break it by pressing buttons and if you need to start again turn it off and on.

You might need to connect the box to your Wi-Fi network by following the prompts. This will be the password on the back of your Wi-Fi box.

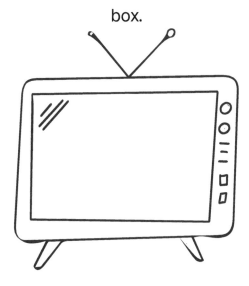

Navigating Your TV Box

Once the box is set up, you'll use its remote to navigate. The remote to control this is separate to the TV one. You could not use a car with a different key, TV's and gadgets are the same.

Here's what to do:

FIRST PRESS THE HOME BUTTON (It may say home or have a image of a house)

Finding Apps:

Look for icons on the screen labeled with names like Netflix, Hulu, or YouTube.
Use the arrow buttons on the remote to highlight the app you want, then press OK or Select.

Signing In:

Some apps require you to sign in with a username and password.
Use the on-screen keyboard to type (your remote will have arrow buttons to move and select letters).

Browsing Content:

Once inside an app, use the arrows to scroll through categories like "Movies," "TV Shows," or "Popular Now."
Highlight something you want to watch and press OK.

Once you have figured this out, you are now a master at the TV!

Switching Back to Regular TV

When you're done using the box and want to return to regular TV:

- Press the Input or Source button on your remote. (See page 13)
- Select TV or the input where your antenna or cable box is connected.

Troubleshooting Tips for Connected Accessories

No Picture or Sound?

Make sure the TV is on the correct input.

Check that the device is turned on and all cables are secure.

Nothing coming up

This may be Wi-Fi Issues - you have to connect to the internet.

This will be found in settings, you will see a button that says setting or has a gear icon.

Double-check your Wi-Fi is connected and reconnect the device to the network.

Remote Not Working?

Replace the batteries or make sure you're pointing it at the box.

Chapter 5: Troubleshooting

Sometimes, things don't go as planned with your TV. Don't worry—this chapter will help you solve common problems step by step.

What to Do When the TV Won't Turn On

Check the Power:
Make sure the power cord is firmly plugged into the wall and the back of the TV.

Try a different outlet if the current one doesn't work.

Look for the Power Light:
Many TVs have a small light on the front. If it's off, the TV isn't getting power.

Use the Power Button:
If the remote doesn't turn the TV on, find the power button on the TV itself (usually near the bottom or back).

Remote Batteries:
Check if the batteries in your remote need to be replaced.

Fixing No Picture or Sound

<u>Check the Input/Source:</u>
Press the Input or Source button on your remote and select the correct input (e.g., HDMI 1 for a streaming box or TV for regular channels).

<u>Make Sure Everything Is Plugged In:</u>

Check that all cables (like HDMI, power cords, or antenna) are securely connected.

<u>Adjust the Volume:</u>

Ensure the volume isn't muted. Press the button that looks like a speaker with a cross through:

Press the Volume Up button on the remote or TV.

<u>Restart the TV:</u>

Turn the TV off, unplug it from the wall, wait 30 seconds, and then plug it back in. Turn it on again.

Solving Remote Control Issues

Replace Batteries:
If the remote isn't working, try replacing the batteries.

Point at the TV:
Make sure you're pointing the remote directly at the TV sensor.

Clean the Remote:
Dust or dirt can block the buttons. Wipe the remote with a dry cloth.

Use the TV Buttons:
If the remote still doesn't work, use the buttons on the TV to navigate until the remote is fixed.

Check you are using the right remote:
If you have more than one remote, make sure you are using the remote for the item you are trying to control.

My TV Is Not What It's Normally Like

If your TV is showing something unusual (like a blank screen or the wrong input), it might need to be switched back to your external TV box.

Press the Input/Source Button:
Look for a button labelled Input, Source, or AV on your remote.

Press it until you see a list of options like HDMI 1, HDMI 2, or TV.

Select the Correct Input:
Use the arrow buttons to highlight the input where your TV box is connected (e.g., HDMI 1).

If you don't know which, just try them all until it works.

Press OK or Enter to select it.

Check the TV Box:

Ensure the box is turned on and connected properly. You should see its home screen or channels on the TV.

What to Do If You're Stuck on a Setting

Sometimes, you might press a button by mistake and end up on a screen or setting you don't recognize. Don't worry—there are easy ways to get back to where you want to be.

Try These Steps:

Press the "Exit" or "Back" Button:

Look for a button on your remote labeled Exit, Back, or Menu.

Press it to leave the setting or menu and return to regular TV.

Switch Inputs:

If you're stuck on a blank screen or the wrong device, press the Input or Source button on your remote.

Select the correct input (e.g., HDMI 1, HDMI 2, or TV) to get back to your shows. (see page 11 for more info)

Turn the TV Off and On Again:

Press the power button on your remote or TV to turn it off.

Wait a few seconds, then turn it back on.

This often resets the TV and takes you back to the main screen.

If All Else Fails:

Ask for Help: If you can't figure it out, a family member, friend, carer, neighbour or even postman might be able to assist.

They may be able to give you tips on what to do in the future - you may benefit from writing these down! There are some note pages at the back of the book if you wish to do so.

Stay Calm: Remember, it's okay to make mistakes. You can always try again, and no harm is done.

Using the approaches mentioned will usually solve the problem and get you back to enjoying your TV. Keep going—you're doing great!

Final Reassurance

If you're still having trouble, don't hesitate to ask for help. Sometimes, a family member, friend, or neighbour can assist. Remember, it's okay to take your time and try again— you're doing great!

This wraps up our guide.

 You're now equipped to handle your TV with confidence.
Enjoy your shows, movies, and everything your TV has to offer!

If you are unsure of what to do, keep going over this guide.

NOTES PAGE

NOTES PAGE

NOTES PAGE

www.ingramcontent.com/pod-product-compliance
Lightning Source LLC
LaVergne TN
LVHW072052060326
832903LV00054B/417